THE ABUNDANCE IS STAGGERING IN FLOWERLAND

THE ABUNDANCE IS STAGGERING IN FLOWERLAND

poems

CYNTHIA HENEBRY

DEAF SHELL PRESS

Published by Deaf Shell Press
www.deafshellpress.com

Printed in the United States of America

ISBN: 979-8-9997937-1-3

Cover Image: Cynthia Henebry
Deaf Shell Press logo and wave drawing: Jesse Timmons

The erotic is a measure between the beginnings of our sense of self
and the chaos of our strongest feelings.

—AUDRE LORDE

CONTENTS

THE ABUNDANCE IS STAGGERING IN FLOWERLAND

THE ABUNDANCE IS STAGGERING IN FLOWERLAND

for Nancy

I wake in pleasure

tangled sheets
the click of the electric kettle

deadheaded sunflowers
in shells I brought back
from the sea

this time I leave

the door to the garden
open

our black house
cat brazenly

walks out

PERSONAL GROWTH

for Gayle

On a rainy Saturday in April
I keep myself
from texting
I miss you—

from asking for what is not given—
from moving away from myself—

from missing the black cat
on a pink rug,

waterdrops falling
onto new
white blossoms.

DID YOU KNOW

for Heather

that in Scotland there's a flower they call gorse?

As in horse,
as in galloping,
as in

I'm going to The Blue Shore soon.

Gorse sounds like a secret message

between friends,
between women,
between poets.

Did you know

that in Scotland they are willing
to be silly with their hearts

broken open?

To give flowers
surprising names and shapes.

When I am in Scotland,
I will be silly too.

STORNOWAY

for Kim

Dark blue
Sea blue
          Harris Tweed blazer—

I'll take that one
          for me
(not him).

THE LAST APPOINTMENT WITH THE COUPLES THERAPIST

for Catherine

He left the love letters behind. His father's ashes,
favorite t-shirts, nail clippers, laminated pass
to the music festival he went to in March.

Still,
I don't think he's moving back.

        I'm moving on.

On the walk to the coffee shop this morning,
yellow flowers

        blooming.

THIS MOTHER'S DAY

for Ellie

I woke to songbirds divebombing
serviceberries, poppies

blooming from the seeds
that Jonny sent me. Sunflowers
growing everywhere,

though I did not plant them.

A WEEK FOR MYSELF

for Holly

Two posies of flowers, the fog.

Spiderwebs flapping
like laundry on the line.

A friend left me a bundle of thyme
when she visited,
I slept with it on my pillow.

Waterlight bouncing
on the ceiling when I woke.

I ENJOY MY OWN COMPANY QUITE A BIT

for Ashley

All through the tidal pools, a glistening—

water pushing into the rocks.
Their boundary like a good mother,
unyielding, not pushing back.

I love them for this, as I love
their brown kelp, my sandy hair,

that pair of clouds
there and then gone.

Ocean,

when you go,
                    take me
                                with you.

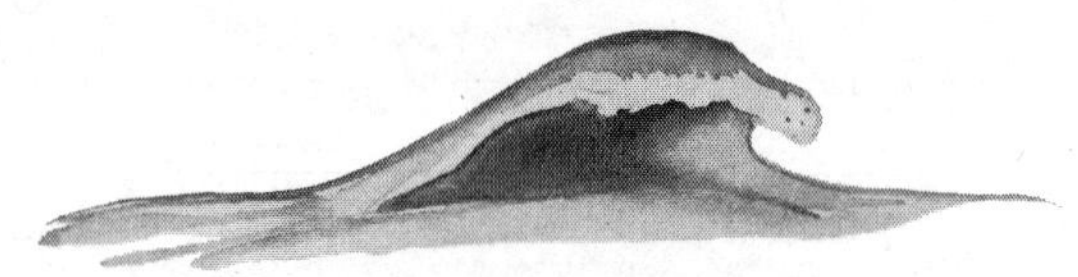

THE SECOND SUMMER

for Sarah

Sometimes, it's muddy in the heart.
And then it rains and rains, and the clay
banks fill with what can only be described
as quenching.

*

In the late afternoons, I go for walks.
Tree roots laid out like tributaries.
I am walking up the architecture
of my—

*

Sadness sloughed off in the first few days.

I deleted the dating app, joined the food co-op,
ate what I wanted when I wanted it,
moved or was fetal when it suited me.

Recharging not collapsing, she said.

*

I opened to grief
then, now
I open

to joy. I won't walk
into the next tragedy, I'll leap.

SUNSET WALK AFTER A CONVERSATION ON ZOOM

for Tawna

Mostly, I walk past the wisdom
of the forest. It's indecipherable.

But there, where the fern
strips itself into stalks, sprouting

from the soil, between mossy rocks.
It's trying to tell me
something.

Breath chuffs from my mouth
in a half hearted effort.

I listen.

IT MUST BE FUN TO BE A DUCK

for Jen

Landing on the water, wings tucked in,
your cute bum skirting the surface,

then nestling into the blue brown
feathers, the color of seaweed at dusk.

You look good alone
or together, either way suits you just fine.

My speckled feet
and legs are no match

for your easy animal nature,
but still.

I rest my limbs along the dock,
let the boats' wake bounce me.

Lucky as you—
well, nearly.

SEAL'S EDGE

for Polly

Once again, the sky pinkens into blue.
Once again, I try to record the day.

Nature, body, injury, armpit,
moss, mouth, water, wine.

My blank face curving,

expressive

as the moon.

(ST)ARS POETICA

for Elese

How can I write a poem about stars?
(How can I not?)

Bright eyes pressed into the darkness,
invisible moon.

I go to sleep, knowing
they are there.

LAST DAY AT THE COTTAGE

for Elizabeth

*white vase with two feathers: one brown, one blue
*my phone
*blue Harris Tweed pencil case the poets gave me filled with shells
*medications, lotions, jewelry
*all of my clothes
*River's clothes
*vacuum cleaner, port-a-crib, purple towel hanging on the white door
*this journal and pencil
*two books by Jim Moore
*small oscillating fan
*this bed and comforter, sheets and pillows
*a green mug with black tea and creamy milk, my belly
*my hands and arms and mouth
*me and possibly my mother, accompanying

water, seaweed, rock, tree, sky

MARRIAGE

for Cornelia

I thought it was one way.
It turned out to be another.

WHAT I WANT

for Bridget

In 1986, I wanted brown leather clogs with braids on them.
I was twelve, and my father walked store after store
with me at Regency Square Mall, searching.
But my feet were too narrow, and I was left wanting.

Now, I want what I have.
Gold bracelet on my right wrist, perfectly circling it.
On my left hand, ringless fingers.

Tea mug in my palm, held by a softening belly.
Black cat sleeping at my side, both of us still
in bed.

I want good friends (I have these),
good cousins (I have these too).
Most importantly, I want time

to spend with them: jokes, dancing,
sympathy. I want us all
to be fluent in sign language.

Not yet, but soon I want a lover.

Someone who worships my body,
who has a body I can worship, too.
I want touch and pleasure and excitement.

I want my sons to walk the world
knowing how much I love them,
not burdened by that love.

I want to remember the Redbud
outside my window when she's gone, the way
her leaves hold water,
glistening on the green.

THE IN-LAWS

for Caroline

I told them I wouldn't come to dinner.

I'm not ready,
it would be awkward,
I want to avoid the stress.

The truth is,

I have pole dancing:
short shorts, bold women,
a new unpracticed self.

*

The marriage is gone.

What even *was* that, I won't
let myself think. That was something, now
this is something else.

School forms, pet walks, the ordinariness
of making dinner, then cleaning it up.

This is what life is, says our old dog,
dreaming away in her sleep.

A shimmering fills the page.

THE COPPER ANNIVERSARY

for Pat

He's not here

—but I am.

A VERY GOOD DAY

for Hannah and Paige

On the eight thousand and thirty sixth day
after our wedding
I woke up,

went for a run, and chatted with a friend
I've known since I was twelve.
My cousin and her young son came over.

We went to the farmer's market.
When we got back
he cracked an egg on his head,
just to see what it feels like.
We laughed and laughed

and laughed.
I went out for dim sum
with other cousins,
devoured pork dumplings and bitter greens.
The restaurant was full with churchgoers.

Afterwards, I meditated,
then talked to another old friend
who was more sad about her children
having gone to college than I was

about my anniversary.
It had been a very good day. Then he texted,
saying he'd left a letter in the mailbox.

I burned it. Next to the bonfire,
the abundance of flowers was staggering—
it was staggering.

AUGUST: FORGIVENESS

for Julia Carr

I hold my anger up
like a peach,
watching it catch the light—

the pink orange cheekiness,
the full bottom heft.

Every color and curve
        a blessing.

I take back its juiciness for myself.

Pleasure drips
from the corners of my mouth,

                I let it.

RESPONSE TO AN EMAIL SAYING HE'S "OPEN TO STAYING LEGALLY MARRIED"

for Amy

I might have been seduced by this once.

How sad to accept such crumbs.

I toss them off, shaking the table cloth in the wind.

It catches the light.

The petals scatter,

joyfully.

SHE SAID PLEASURE'S NOT A LOOK, IT'S A FEELING

for Nia

Like the press of palms
on a cold metal pole,
          bottom extended—

I was the oldest in the room,
so what? We all came

with our perceived inadequacies,
we all wanted to be free.

As free as she was,

perched on impossible stilettos,
gaze turned inward,

          her whole body
                    turning
                              out, out, out.

IN SEPTEMBER I STARTED LIVING THE LIFE I ACTUALLY HAVE

for Annie

So many things that could be sad
aren't,
        now—

changing my emergency contact

sole responsibility of the animals

this morning cup of tea.

The other side of the bed—

open window,
            beyond.

This collection of poems is for Nancy. For Polly and Holly and Heather. For Daisy, Mary Jane, and Andy. For three Virginias and Ingrid. Dorothy. For Jen and Gayle and Bridget. For Joanna and Amy and Laura. Andrea, Amina and Margaret. For three beloved Ashleys, and all my dear Eliz/sabeths. For Annie, all Carolines, Rachel, Hannah and Paige. For Julia Carr. For all three Reginas, Julia, Nina, and both Suzannes. For Dottie and Jaishri, Callie and two Nicoles. Sarah and Jalisa, Kiran and Vanessa. Mara. These lines are for Katie and Rose. Lisa and Marlene, Marjolein and Donna. For my namesake Cynthia, and her second youngest sister Kathryn. This is for Diane. For Ellie, Alicia, and Marsha. Patsy, Louise, Carrington, Sarah, Stacey, Patti, Katherine, Meg. Cassandra. These words honor Shelley. Konda and Smiley, Marian and Elspeth. Stacy. This is for Kim and Catherine, and all my Poetry Forge sisters. For Sandra and Mary Anne and Magee. This collection is for Tawna. For Valley and for Nia. These poems are for Patricia. For my mother and my grandmothers, and all the men we love. These poems are for *you*.

ENJOY.

The Abundance Is Staggering in Flowering is typset in Garamond Premier Pro. Book design by Lindsay Lake. Composition by Bookmobile Design & Digital Publisher Services, Minneapolis, Minnesota. Manufactured by Bookmobile on acid-free, 100 percent postconsumer waste paper.